Knocking from the Inside

By Patricia Florin

Long Journey Home Press

Williams, Oregon

Knocking from the Inside

Long Journey Home Press
Williams, Oregon
www.PatriciaFlorin.info

First edition: 2016

ISBN 978-0-9965823-2-2

Manufactured in the United States of America

10 9 8 7 6 5 4 3 2 1

For my sister seekers,
here's to finding it.

I have lived on the lip of insanity
Wanting to know reasons
Knocking on a door, it opens
I have been knocking from the inside!
~ Rumi

Knocking from the Inside

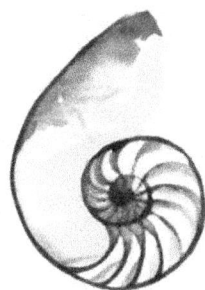

SEARCHING

She thought herself an ordinary woman—
married, raising three children—living an
ordinary life. In her daylight hours she
prepared meals, chauffeured kids, and
worked at the computer. At night, after her
husband and kids were asleep, she would
pull a small wooden chair up to the window,
look out at the trees shaking their branches at
the stars, and wonder: *What is all this? What
am I?*

When she stopped looking out the window,
she lit a candle and sat at the pine table. She
reached for her notebook and, with no plan,
poured out her confusion. And, sometimes,
when she finished, she sat back and laughed,
for in the deepest, closest part of herself, she
could feel the answer.

THE TOKEN

Put in play,
I am moved into place
to become another,
clay that feelings mold
into drama.

Then I am put back
wait to be
taken out again
and used in
another game.

Outside Looking Out

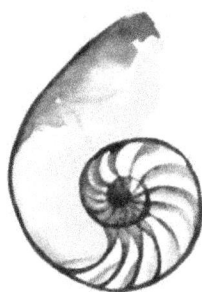

WOMAN OFF THE COAST OF FIFTY

Frantic
yesterday's Town Darling
plucks half-inch hairs
sprouting from her chin.

Distraction dismisses her words, and
she must concoct long, sketchy
    descriptions
of simple things with simple names.

She feeds her spirit Scotch and Cheez-Its,
cools herself in front of the open freezer,
and takes in low-down bass boys —
Cohen, Brown, Redbone.

        Estrogen, progesterone,
        soy, yam, yoga,
        moisturizers,
        lubricators —
        constitutional
        re-creators.
        Don't worry, dear,
        help's on the shelf.

Honed by decades of duty
she barks caution
    to youths
    giggling their way into
    happiness and trouble
watches over
    aged parents
    frail, frustrated, fearful
and tends
    the tempers of men.

Maybe,
somewhere
off the coast of fifty,
    the seas will level
    and the current carry
    this daughter of Gaia
    to a soft sand shore
    lined with easy
    chairs and soft-hued umbrellas.

    Caressed by warm breezes
    she will slumber
    under palm trees.

    When she wakes, she will
    sip tropical drinks
    settle into her crone body
    tote up her heart's accumulation
    mine her hard-won wisdom
    and wait for understanding
    to show up
    before she returns
    to stake a new place in the world
    where she can choose
    to be either
        invisible,
        the batty lady in 2B,
        or a grand dame of life.

Waiting Game

Two sprouting girls
cloaked by a blanket
giggle and play with toy horses.

Eighteen-year-old man-boy
voice thick with bravado
holes up in his cave
to socialize with his
computer.

Timeworn in-laws
tuck in
a few blocks away
as the inevitable approaches.

Husband out working his
dream
leaving space
where his heart used to be.

I sit in the dark corner
and type others' words
as uncertainty runs
through my veins, and

out the window, buds,
drunk on green,
offer themselves
to the swollen belly
of a dark gray sky.

FREELANCE TYPIST

What happens to your thoughts
when they pass through the typist?
> *In response to your letter…*
> *My payment is three months late*
> > *because…*
> *My parents came over on a boat…*
> *If you would just listen, I wouldn't*
> > *have to write this…*
> *Once upon a time…*
> *Enclosed please find my*
> > *proposal*
> > *poem*
> > *resume*
> > *essay*
> > *transcript*
> > *manuscript*
> > *wife's obituary*

She searches your confusion
senses your intention
finds the words
as her fingers make the sound of
    heavy raindrops
and letters roll across the screen.
The printer clicks and whines
and delivers your words.

She takes your money,
walks you to the door,
returns to her keyboard and screen,
and begins new work
as your words,
still whispering to her,
layer pieces of your truth among her own.

CRITIQUED

New input thrashes about
sorts itself
deliberates
breathes light into my confusion.

Oh. Crap.

I plan a memorial service
for the flawed anatomy
of my craftsmanship
and two years gone.
Shred all that paper,
cry over the bytes and hours,
and wait for class
in the next idea.

GORILLA IN THE LIVING ROOM

There's a gorilla
in our living room.
Black-waxy bulk,
eyes dark pools that watch
and blink.

You and I
walk around it
pretend it isn't there
while this dark, hairy
intelligence
waits for us
to listen.

Maybe if we're
  patient
      it'll go
         away.
           Phhtt!

"It'll Be Okay"

Angry wind bullies trees
on the other side of the window
as I sit with my father-in-law.
His deathbed flesh
is like a stubborn oak leaf
dangling at winter's end.
Over his head
dim light offers the only softness.

Ignore the smells,
the groans,
the heavy breathing
as he tries to bellow fire
back into his body.

The nurse tells me to
hold his hand, speak to him,
he'll hear me.

I love you.
Thank you for everything,
especially for your son.
It's okay to go.

That last is a lie.
It's not okay.
Nothing has been okay
since the surgeon's scalpel
nicked the life out of him.

* * *

Five months and fifteen hundred
        miles ago
another father, another death.
Unconscious for days, he had snuck back,

11

opened his eyes and looked around.

When his eyes landed upon me
he tried to smile.
His lip split.
I swabbed his dry mouth with the
    pink sponge,
offered water,
leaned the straw so he could suck.

I told him I had to go home.

His eyes smiled, then darkened,
a moan rumbled his chest,
his jaw struggled to work.
He pierced me with his
I-know-when-you're-lying look
and said,
"I'm never going to see you again,
    am I?"

I had wanted to sneak past this moment,
pretend this was just another goodbye,
then escape before he could understand.

But he knew.
Of course he knew, this dear man
who had worked seven days a week
and raised eight children,
who, when I was twelve, helped me
    read the Constitution,
explained it line by line,
who never understood my thinking
but held my hand as I labored with
    my firstborn.

I could not yield,
could not tell him *Yes,*
your life is almost over,
and I will miss you so much.
It would break us both.

So I whispered,
"It'll be okay."

Another deathbed lie.

DRUNKEN COMPUTER TALK

I am drunk and deleting icons from
    my desktop.
Don't need 'em.
World's too fast
and there're all these silly things I
    never use
floatin' in front of me.
What do I care about *Content Transfer*
    and *ReadyComm*?
What do I know about figging my sys?
Or is that syssing my fig?
But I'm keeping *Quick Time Player*.
I like quick time. And play.

I'm gonna make new icons.
Useful ones.
There'll be a "Press-here-for-the-food-
    of-your-choice-to-roll-out-of-the-
    DVD-tray" icon.
How about a "Have-to-pee-but-too-
    busy-to-leave-the-computer" icon?
I want an "Instantly-piss-off-that-rude-
    person" icon. Just press it, and voila!
    Annoyer becomes annoyee.
There'll be a "Figure-it-out-for-me" icon
right next to the "Figure-it-out-for-
    yourself" icon.
What I really need, though, is a
    "Reboot-my-head" icon.

Kneeling on Hard Judgment

I look in on you
your locked-tight world
bring you a story.
You take the book,
read the cover,
       pronounce, "Evil!"
and cast it into the fire,
then pick up your book of Scripture,
and thump on it.

I look in on you
your locked-tight world
slip you cake.
You laugh thank-you,
touch your tongue
to the dark sweetness,
then spit it out and jam it down the sink.
    You explain, "This is how
      the Devil works."

I look in on you
your locked-tight world
point to the sky, eternity's canvas,
point to the trees, the here and now.
You claim it is a trick,
tell me you have the future
all locked up,
then drop to your knees and beg,
      "Come be saved with me!"
I blow you a kiss,
walk away.

I look in on you
your locked-tight world
where you kneel on hard judgment
and pray to be not
what you think you are—a "sinner."
I sigh, sink to the grass,
and count stars.

I Want to Tuck My Baby In

I want to tuck my baby in
but she's out
with her
boyfriend

Her father burrows —
eyes distant
face gray —
low in the recliner

TV's brassy cackles
and lashing lights
score our thought-tickers:
 We said we wouldn't worry
 Did we tell her enough? Too much?

The dog's foot thumps
as he scratches himself

I pace

Ten-'til-curfew
the door whooshes open
revealing our baby
with a woman's body
and a lover's smile

SUSHI AND MOCHA

In this place…

     where light cannot find a foothold,
     sour stinks steal air,
     paneling peels off the walls,
     and drawers and cabinets crumble
        to rubble,
     rain on the metal roof
     out-rackets the thunder,
       The roof is leaking again
     tequila bottle magnifies the mouse
     which leers, "I dare you!"
     dog, nose to floor,
     drives herself mad
     as she follows the movements
     of the creature that lives below us,
     cold and heat
     play sadistic games,
     drafts blow in dust,
     and the only hint
     of the previous owner—
        that white lab coat
        on a wire hanger
        in the closet with the sticking door
        and a white countertop
        riddled with slashes

…in this place
I sit in bed,
sip homemade mocha,
nibble leftover sushi,

and listen to NPR
   Renee Montagne and Steve Inskeep —
   New York and the Capital
in my Oregon trailer
on this dark, cold
five-thirty A.M.

THOUGHT TRAPS

Thought-traps.
I create them,
and watch as they
embellish themselves
in this housewife life of
laundry, making meals, paying bills,
     vacuuming.
They break in, say
        This isn't enough.
        Go out in the world,
        do something that <u>*matters*</u>*.*

And I feel small as they
flog me with their sense of
a life wasted on ordinary tasks.

When I give my mind to that Other,
the one who
        feels the smooth brush of the
            broom across bare floor,
        takes the dog into her arms and
            nuzzles it,
        feels the simple joy of transmuting
            flour, butter, vegetables, and
            spices into a meal,
        stands outside and lets the sky talk
            to her heart
        while the earth enlivens her desire,
she shows that nothing,
is ever
        ordinary.

ASLANT

Today is a
tip-me-over day
aslant in gray gravity.

Today is an
airport terminal day
out of time
out of space
in no place.

Today is a
hospital waiting room day
No promises.

Today is an
empty bottle of a day.

How Long?

Death snugged up to me,
offered a conspiratorial wink.
I nearly jumped
out of my skin.
I asked,
    "How long have you been here?"
He chuckled.

Outside Looking In

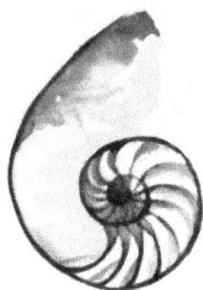

UNCERTAIN

Death slapped me,
snapped me out of sheltered sleep,
and dumped me in this new town,
which looks just like the old one
except that I am changed,
uncertain as I tend this life
because I suspect
it does not belong to me.

And many times a day
I collapse
    at the hand of doubt
    in the heart of despair
    in the restraint of failure
    in thoughts believed
    in love forgotten.

When I let myself fall into
the embrace of silence,
my chest rises
on windless breath.
If I release to this,
a softer grace sweeps me up.
But if I grasp,
I drown.

I feel like a toddler
running one step
ahead of gravity.

BLISS-BLOCKED

Grace tugs, pulls,
drags me through the muck and pain
my beliefs create
until I cry out,
    I give up!

And she snatches me up,
drops me into emptiness,
where I float, wonder,
fret at loneliness,
wait for the magic and bliss.

Hah!

At Depth

Dropping through space,
reentering atmosphere,
resistance streaks the stars

Impact smacks flesh and bone,
threshes mind from body,
soul from flesh

Cold sea-darkness seeps in,
shapes and forms
dart and weave

Breathe,
wait for a lifeline.

COVENANT

Do you know how
lonely it is
knocking around
inside this flesh
captive to
what these eyes see,
these ears hear,
and this body senses and smells?

Can my heart be joined
in this forlorn love-desert?

What was it I had promised to do?
It had better be worth this.

MINDING THE STILL

Tender Heart
cast into the night
and the arms of a blizzard.

Fearful Heart
lives behind concrete
and barbed wire.
Nothing gets in
and nothing gets out but
growls.

Drunken Heart
rolls down the road
tipping into taverns
getting kicked out
amid harsh laughs
and confusion.

Desert Heart
crackles in isolation
to incinerate pain and
burn free
of the past.

Romantic Heart
sneaks out at night
to make passes
and sing ballads,
then shuts down with dawn.

Where is the Heart
that minds
this still of experience?

AM I DREAMING?

I do not know what I am.
That is the truest thing I can say.

Now what?
Make dinner,
feed the horses,
build a fire for the night,
look at my man
who naps in the chair
instead of going to bed
because he did not want to give up
    the day.

I walk the dog and wonder at the stars,
sparkling pinpoints in the emptiness.
Do they know what they are?
Does this little animal,
sniffing the hard ground,
know what he is?

Day after day
we play out time
then gather in the bed,
pull in, close down this reality,
and fall into another.

HONK IF YOU'RE BUDDHA

Drivin' along
wonderin' where I'm goin'
and why.
Seem to have forgotten
   … something.

Buddha passes me
smilin', bobbin' his head
to the bass-blasting radio
of the red convertible he guides with
two fingers across the bottom of the
   steerin' wheel slidin' over his girth.
With his other fleshy hand he honks
   and waves
as he pulls past.
The yellow words on his purple bumper
   sticker:

ALL ROADS LEAD TO WHERE YOU'RE GOING.

Truth will associate
with anyone.
It can't help itself.

Inside Looking Out

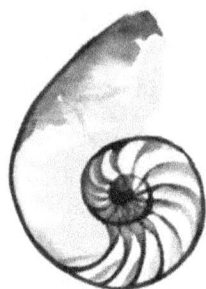

Dear One,
Are you thirsty?
Hungry?
Misplaced your spirit
        somewhere along the way?
Wait, don't tell me ...
        you lost your key again
            didn't you?

Now?

Did you know
I wait
on the back stoop
of your consciousness?

I keep getting
mis-ID'd at the door
as a pipedream.
The bouncer's been bullying all

possibilities not belonging
to the mundane
and about-facing them.
Let me in!
Let me in.

Beauty waits for me
to wake
so It can show me
Its heart.

Death breathes
up my spine
stinging me to life.

I loved you lifetimes ago
and find you again
today
drinking life
from the same cup.

Shall we dance?

KNOCKING FROM THE INSIDE

As I crawled out from under the ignorance
that crowded my heart,
I sensed my way
along fear's underbelly.
Time and again it pricked me,
then recoiled, warning:
    Don't touch me.
    I protect you.

For decades I pushed past its warnings
so I could move to a new land,
practice yoga, meditate, do tai chi,
read books with claims of wisdom,
sit alone,
wait,
wonder.

One early autumn morning
a clarifying thought moved in:
    I wished to know Truth.
Within hours
I was wheeled into the ER,
anaphylactic,
able to move only one toe.
Cheap trick.

I floated in darkness,
waited,
talked to it,
told it I would stay
because I wanted to know what is true
even if it was only this.

I heard nothing,
felt nothing

nothing.

That was my answer.

Until many months later
sitting in my living room
in my mind's eye —
a brain flash.

And another.

Two ideas partnered as One:
IT IS ALL TRUE   NOTHING IS TRUE

And I laughed so hard!

All I ever had to do was
let go —
no beliefs, no labels, no expectations —
and, clear-hearted, watch
as Life lived Itself
through this vehicle I called "me."

SHADOW DANCE

Moon presses through trees
to throw pebbles of light
at my window —
                    "Dance with me."
She offers up another
as partner, undulating,
            pulsing, gliding, spinning,
                    twin asps
                        waving and weaving.
Wind's cool caresses slip
                under our skirts,
                    coaxing our
            blush.
        Grass and stones
        echo our steps
        down
    to Earth,
who has been
    waiting
to take us in.
        Our hearts pulse
                    joy
                and send laughter
                            to the
                                Moon.

THE KISS

What you thought
was the sting of death
was actually
the Kiss of God.
We laugh with the joy
of a parent
whose child just noticed
the stars.

Inside Looking In

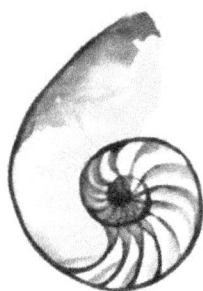

Waking up
is like walking a tightrope.
Blindfolded.
Without a rope.

BECOMING

I sit on the bony lap of Old Age
look it in its clouded eye, and say:

> You don't scare me.
> You don't disgust me.
> You don't bore me.
> You don't even fool me.
> You fascinate me.

What am I becoming?

THE UNWRAPPING

I don't even care what I will become.
That threat has lost its weight.
All that matters is
    an inch that way,
    small breaths finding
    the space between,
    as I search for a hole.

In this body's pain
love unwraps itself
takes pieces of what used to be me
and tosses them into the sky.

Consciousness outlives the body?
How would I know?
I am drops of ink on paper.
Ask the paper.

IN THE CHAMBER

I run backward through the marketplace
of thoughts mating
as I look for the IN door,
where I know something true
waits.
I knock.
The door disappears.
Cool darkness ushers me in.

Welcome.

I cannot see the speaker
only a tree.

Recognize it?

I do.
Silver boughs
bear moments—
    The scent of almond blossoms
    The rawness of the mental hospital
    Him taking my hand
    Warming in summer's breath
    Playing with my babies
    Maple trees' autumn show
    Gravity revising my back
    Frosty breath hanging midair
    Heart and mind ruptured by grief
Life jewels
shining and shaped by Seeing.

Take this back with you.

Then what?

Remind yourself.

ALWAYS HERE

The kiss I throw out to the world
whirls around
and returns to my lips:

> *Here it is ... here...*
> *close your eyes and see*
> *truth*
> *is always*
> *right*
> *here.*

Love came over today
seeking a cup
for her tea.
I gave her me.

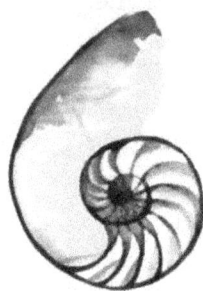

ACKNOWLEDGEMENTS

For their patient reading and rereading of
these poems, a big thank you to Addie Green,
Deborah Rothschild, Dolores de Leon, Ellen
Gardner Hauck, Melissa Brown, Bert
Anderson, Herb Long, Heather Murphy,
Gabriela Eaglesome. Special thanks to
Dorothy Vogel and Honora NiAodagain for
your extra thorough review.

Thank you, Marilyn Joy, for sticking this out
with me and lighting the way when I was lost.

Thank you, Susan Edmonds, for believing in
this work.

And always, thank you, Steve, for creating
the opportunity for me to dream and write.

Patricia Florin lives with her husband in southern Oregon, where she writes, edits, and helps tend their farm.

www.PatriciaFlorin.info

Photograph courtesy Ellen Gardner Hauck

www.ingramcontent.com/pod-product-compliance
Lightning Source LLC
Chambersburg PA
CBHW020955030426
42339CB00005B/119